RICHARD MICO

The Four-Part Consort Music

edited by Meredith Tyler

in memory of John Bennett

CONTENTS

INTRODUCTION ii
EDITORIAL NOTES iii
CRITICAL COMMENTARY iv

FOUR-PART FANCIES

1	(VdGS no. 14)	2
2	(VdGS no. 13)	4
3	(VdGS no. 15)	6
4a	(VdGS no. 17)	8
4b	(VdGS no. 17)	10
5	(VdGS no. 16)	12
6	(VdGS no. 1)	14
7	(VdGS no. 2)	16
8	(VdGS no. 3)	18
9	(VdGS no. 4)	20
10	(VdGS no. 5)	23
11	(VdGS no. 6)	25
12	(VdGS no. 7)	27
13	(VdGS no. 8)	29
14	(VdGS no. 9)	31
15	(VdGS no. 10)	34
16	(VdGS no. 11)	36
17	(VdGS no. 12)	38
18	(VdGS no. [18])	40
19	(VdGS no. [19])	42

FOUR-PART PAVANS

1	(VdGS no. 1)	44
2	(VdGS no. 2)	46
3	(VdGS no. 3)	48
4	(VdGS no. 4)	50

ISBN-10: 0 9517524 4 8; ISBN-13: 9780951752449. Fretwork Editions, London
General Editors: Bill Hunt & Julia Hodgson.
1st edition © 1992, 2nd edition © 1997

INTRODUCTION

Until recently, very little was known about Richard Mico's life. Early references to Mico are meagre but they suggest that Mico was regarded as one of the leading consort composers of the time. Christopher Simpson mentioned Mico briefly in his *Compendium of Practical Music* of 1665 during his discussion of "fancies of 6, 5, 4 and 3 parts, intended commonly for viols".[1]

> Of this sort you may see many compositions made heretofore in England by Alfonso Ferabosco, Coperario, Lupo, White, Ward, Mico, Dr. Colman, and many more now deceased. Also by Mr. Jenkins, Mr. Locke, and divers other excellent men, doctors and bachelors in music yet living.[2]

In his *Memoires of Musick* of 1728, Roger North also honoured Mico by including him in a list of "those authors of musicall composition whose performances gained to the nation the credit of excelling the Itallians in all but the vocall."[3] However, because the works of these composers were lost in "oblivion" by this time, North apparently knew little more than their names. For those readers who were curious, he suggested that in

> some gentlemens old collections, not yet rotten . . . one might find some of Alfonso Ferabosco, Coperario, (anglice Cooper) Lupo, Mico, Est, and divers others, especially of one Mr. John Jenkins, whose musicall works are more voluminous, and in the time more esteemed then all the rest, and now lye in the utmost contempt.[4]

The editor of North's manuscript in 1846 added a footnote to the above quotation, informing the reader that Mico "flourished in the reign of James and his successor, but no particulars of him are known."[5]

It was not until 1977 that a detailed account of Mico's life was published, based on the extensive research into seventeenth-century manuscript sources by John Bennett and Pamela Willetts.[6] Their research revealed details of Mico's dates, family and career. Richard Mico was born about 1590 and was the eldest of three sons of Walter Mico and Margery Awdrey of Taunton in Somerset. Mico held two major positions during his musical career. The first began in 1608, when Mico entered the service of the Petre family of Essex as a resident musician. The Petre family was a wealthy Catholic family, owning two main residences in Essex: Thorndon Hall (near Brentwood) and Ingatestone Hall. Mico's duties would have included looking after the music for Chapel and teaching music to the children of the household. Though born of Protestant parents, Mico probably converted to Catholicism whilst working for the Petres. William Byrd was a close friend of the Petre family and a frequent visitor to Thorndon Hall. It is therefore likely that Mico came into considerable contact with Byrd during this period.

The second phase of Mico's musical career began in 1630 when Mico entered the service of Queen Henrietta Maria, the Catholic wife of Charles I. A surviving acquittance book from the Queen's household records that from Michaelmas 1630 onwards Mico was receiving fees of thirty pounds per quarter. A later acquittance book includes the marginal note "Richard Mico organist," suggesting that Mico was the successor of Richard Dering who had been Henrietta Maria's organist since her marriage in 1625 and who died towards the end of March 1630.

With the outbreak of Civil War in 1642, the Queen's household disbanded and Henrietta Maria made a hasty escape to Holland. Probably several of her French musicians left for France at the same time. However Mico appears to have remained in London. It is not known how Mico supported himself during the Civil War and the early 1650s, but it is known that by December 1658, he was receiving a life annuity of twenty pounds from William, Fourth Lord Petre. According to a parish register from St. Paul's Church, Covent Garden, London, "Mr. Richard Micoe" was buried in the Church on 10 April 1661.

Music by Mico existed only in manuscript sources in the seventeenth century. The distribution of those manuscripts which have survived to the present day indicates that his music must have enjoyed quite a wide circulation. Thirty-nine compositions are known to have been written by Mico, all of which are for viols. However, there are four more compositions for viols which have been confidently attributed to Mico on the basis of their position in the sources in which they occur and their style.[7] A fifth composition appears to be an earlier version of one of his four-part fancies.[8] This brings the total number of pieces by Mico to forty-four. Mico's four-part compositions, which are presented in this edition, comprise more than half of his surviving output, the remainder being consort music for two, three and five viols.

In their research, Bennett and Willetts uncovered specimens of Mico's signature from different periods of his life, enabling a rough dating of some of his music. They suggest that Mico probably wrote most of his consort music during his long period of service for the Petres in Essex (1608–30). The Petre household is known to have had a chest of viols and it is likely that as an employed musician, Mico would have been called upon to produce consort music for the family to play. The fact that the Petre chest lacked a second bass is possibly the reason Mico did not compose for more than five viols.

---

[1] Christopher Simpson, *A Compendium of Practical Music in Five Parts*, ed. Phillip J. Lord (Oxford: Basil Blackwell, 1970, reprint of 2nd rev. ed., 1667), 77.
[2] Ibid., 78.
[3] Roger North, *Memoires of Musick*, MS [1728], ed. Edward F. Rimbault (London: George Bell, 1846), 83.
[4] Ibid., 84-5.
[5] Ibid., 85.
[6] John Bennett and Pamela Willetts, "Richard Mico," *Chelys* 7 (1977): 24-46.
[7] Four-part Fancies nos.18 and 19 (VdGS nos.[18] and [19]); five-part Fancies VdGS nos.3 and 4.

EDITORIAL NOTES

Sources
This edition of the four-part fancies and pavans of Richard Mico is based on London Royal College of Music MS 1197 (abbreviated as Lcm). Its selection as the principal source for the edition was based on the fact that it includes Mico's signature on the title page of each part-book and is the only source exclusively devoted to his four-part works. The editor has consulted all known sources and noted all significant variant readings in the Critical Commentary.

Abbreviations used for Manuscript Sources of Richard Mico's Four-Part Works
London: Royal College of Music
    Lcm   Music MS 1197 [Principal source in this edition]
London: British Library
    Lbl   Additional MS 31423
    Lms   Madrigal Society MSS G.33-36
Oxford: Christ Church Library
    Och1 Music MSS 353-56
    Och2 Music MSS 517-20

Numbering
The numbering of the pavans and fancies in this edition is based on the order of pieces in the autograph set of part-books, Royal College of Music MS 1197 (Lcm). This numbering differs from that adopted by Ernst H. Meyer[1] for the fancies (and subsequently adopted by the Viola da Gamba Society[2]) which was based on the order of pieces in the part-books, Oxford, Christ Church Library, Music MSS 353-56 (Och1). In the present edition, the Viola da Gamba Society numbering is indicated on the contents page and in the Critical Commentary using the abbreviation "VdGS no.".

Titles
No titles are present in any of the sources except the Royal College of Music MS 1197. In this manuscript, each part has an inscription on the inner cover, "Pavans and fancies of 4 parts. Rich: Mico," which is believed to be written by the composer himself. The outer covers have a similar inscription written in a different hand: "Pavans and fancyes of 4 parts composed by Richard Mico." Three pieces within the set are given titles as follows, (using the manuscript numbering):

No.1 bears the title "Pavan" in each part. [Pavan no.1 in this edition].

No.7 is labelled "Fancy" in parts I and II only. [Fancy no.3 in this edition].

No.14 is entitled "Ut re mi fa" in parts I and II only. [Fancy no.10 in this edition].

These titles appear to have been added by the same person who wrote on the outer covers. This hand has not yet been identified. The term "fancy" is used in this edition rather than "fantasia" because this is the term used by the composer himself.

Attributions
When the term "attributed" is used in the commentary, it refers either to an attribution appearing with the individual piece concerned or to a blanket attribution found at the beginning of the source. For example, Royal College of Music MS 1197 has a title page at the beginning of each part-book attributing all the music it contains to Richard Mico. There are no blanket attributions in the other sources.

The Unattributed Fancies nos. 18 and 19
Fancies 18 and 19 have been included in this edition despite the fact that they do not appear in the principal source, Royal College of Music MS 1197. These two four-part pieces are unique to one source: Oxford, Christ Church Library, Music MSS 517-20, and are surrounded by works known to be by Mico. On the grounds of context and style, the two fancies have been attributed to Mico by the Viola da Gamba Society. Research for this edition has revealed no significant inconsistencies in style, thereby supporting the attributions.

Instrumentation
In this edition, parts are labelled *viols 1-4* to reflect the non-specific designations given in the sources. Parts for *viols 1, 3* and *4* can be confidently assigned to treble, tenor and bass viols respectively, whilst the range of the *viol 2* part suggests either a treble or a tenor viol. In Royal College of Music MS 1197, the parts are identified on the title pages as *Cantus, Altus, Tenor* and *Bassus* (inner covers) and *Superius, Medius, Tenor* and *Bassus* (outer covers). In Oxford, Christ Church, Music MSS 353-56, part I of the first fancy in the sequence is labelled *Cantus* and part IV of the same fancy is labelled *Bassus*. In Madrigal Society MSS G.33-36, each part of the first piece in the sequence is labelled respectively *Cantus, Altus, Tenor* and *Bassus*.

Accidentals
In reading the sources, accidentals have been taken to follow the seventeenth-century convention of each applying only to the note it precedes, except in the following circumstances: (a) When the principal source or the concordances have the same note repeated consecutively, and supply an accidental for the first note but not for the repeated note(s), the accidental is assumed to apply to the repeated note(s); (b) In cadential figures where a sharp or natural is given for the first note but not for repetitions of that note later in the figure, the accidental is assumed to apply also to the latter. In this edition, all accidentals (original and editorial) follow the modern convention of lasting the whole bar unless cancelled. Redundant accidentals have been tacitly omitted. Obsolete accidentals (for example, the use of sharps to cancel flats) are modernised. Editorial accidentals are placed above the note and these are mostly to cancel the effect of an original accidental occurring earlier in the bar.

Clefs
Treble (G2), alto (C3) and bass (F4) clefs have been retained whenever they occur in the principal source. All other clefs used in the principal source have been altered to one of the above in order to facilitate modern performance. The original clefs used in the principal source are indicated on the prefatory staves. Clefs used in the concordances are noted in the Commentary when they differ from those of the principal source.

Key-Signatures
Original key-signatures are retained, except in Fancy no.3 where each part has been transcribed using the same key-signature rather than employing the partial key-signatures of the principal source.

Time-Signatures
Royal College of Music MS 1197 and Oxford, Christ Church Library, Music MSS 517–20 use ₵ for their time-signatures whereas British Library Additional MS 31423, Madrigal Society MSS G.33–36 and Oxford, Christ Church Library, Music MSS 353–56 all use ₵. To avoid confusion, the modern time-signature 4/2 has been used in this edition. The only exception is Pavan no.1, where the time signature 6/2 has been employed in two bars in order to indicate the original note values (and therefore, strain lengths) of the principal source.

Prefatory Staves
The principal source's original clefs, key-signatures, time-signatures and the first sounding note of each part are shown on the prefatory staves. Ranges of parts (which are editorial) are given before the editorial time-signature.

Barring
Regular breve barring occurs in the *cantus* part of Royal College of Music MS 1197 in the four pavans and the first eight fancies but does not occur in the other parts (except for part II of Fancy no.10). The barlines appear to have been added later, probably by the same hand that wrote the inscriptions on the outer covers. London British Library Additional MS 31423 is the only other source which includes barlines, reflecting its later origin. This source has regular semibreve barring in all the parts throughout the manuscript. The regular breve barring in this edition is editorial.

Note-Values
Original note-values are retained, with the exception of final notes of the fancies which are standardized to fit the barring; these changes are not noted in the commentary. Beaming has been tacitly regularized to reflect the minim beat. Where necessary, stem directions and notation of rests are altered to conform with modern notational practice without comment.

Editorial Suppression of Material in the Principal Source
A note or rest enclosed in square brackets indicates that the reading in the principal source has been suppressed. Original readings are cited in the Commentary.

[1] Ernst H. Meyer, *Die Mehrstimmige Spielmusik des 17. Jahrhunderts in Nord- und Mitteleuropa* (Kassel: Barenreiter, 1934), 160.
[2] Gordon J. Dodd, comp., *Thematic Index of Music for Viols*, (London: Viola da Gamba Society of Great Britain, 1980–).

CRITICAL COMMENTARY

References
In the references below, bar numbers are shown in Arabic numerals; parts are numbered in Roman numerals (the uppermost part being I); the number of the note in the bar is given in Arabic numerals; exact pitch is indicated by the Helmholtz system (where middle C is c' and the octave below middle C reads from c-b, and the octave below that from C-B); references are separated by an oblique stroke. References follow the format: bar number, part, number of note in bar (or indication of rest), reading or other comment, and the source(s) in which this occurs using the abbreviations given in the Editorial Notes. (If a note is tied across the bar then this counts as two notes, so that the tied note in the new bar is designated as note 1.)

The following abbreviations are employed in the Commentary:

b = breve; $sb.$ = dotted semibreve; sb = semibreve; $m.$ = dotted minim
m = minim; $c.$ = dotted crotchet; c = crotchet; $q.$ = dotted quaver
q = quaver; sq = semiquaver; o = no accidental; om. = omitted
k-s = key-signature; t-s = time-signature

Fancy no.1 (VdGS no.14)
Principal Source: Lcm (attributed).
Concordances: Lms (unattributed), Och1 (attributed), Och2 (unattributed).
Part IV is written in F4 clef in Och1, Och2 and Lms.

6 I 3,4: *c.*f', *qg'* (Och1) / 8 III 3: a (Lms) / 8 IV 2-3: *me*-flat (Och1, Och2) / 9 IV 1 - *m*-rest: *sb*G (Och2) / 10 I 6-7: *md*" (Och2) / 12 I 1-2: slurred (Lms) / 12 IV 6 - 13 IV 1: tie om. (Lms) / 16 I 3 - 17 I 1: *sb*a' tied to *sb*a', *sb*a' (Och2) / 17 I 1: *sb*a' *sb*a' (Och1) / 17 III 1: o (Och1) / 23 III 4: o (Och1) / 24 III 3: *qe*' *qc*' *qd*' *qe*' (Och1) / 28 II 6 - 29 II 1: tie om. (Och1) / 28 IV 1: *sb*d *sb*d (Lms) / 29 I 1-3: slurred (Lms) / 29 III 1: *ma ca* (Lms) / 29 IV 4: G (Och2); *sbg sb*G (Lms).

Fancy no.2 (VdGS no.13)
Principal Source: Lcm (attributed).
Concordances: Lbl (unattributed), Och1 (attributed), Och2 (unattributed).
Part I is missing in Lbl.
Part II is written in C1 clef in Och1 and Och2; C2 clef in Lcm and Lbl.
Part IV is written in F4 clef in Och1, Och2 and Lbl.

2 II 1,2: *cd*', *cd*" (Och1) / 4 I 3: natural (Och2) / 5 IV 4-5: *mg* (Lbl, Och2) / 6 III 6: sharp (Lbl, Och1) / 7 IV 3: o (Och1) / 9 II 7: o (Och1) / 9 III 3: o (Och1) / 9 III 5: o (Och1, Och2) / 11 II 8: o (Lbl) / 16 IV 1-3: *c.*b-flat *q*b-flat *q*b-flat *q*a (Och1) / 21 II 3: o (Och1, Och2) / 21 II 7-8: *sb*a' (Och1) / 21 III 3,4: *c., q* (Och1) / 21 III 4: natural (Lbl, Och2) / 21 III 9: *ce*' (Och1) / 21 IV 3: o (Lbl, Och1) / 22 I *sb*-rest: om. (Och2) / 22 II 5: a' (Och1) / 22 IV 1: D (Och1) / 24 I 3: o (Och1, Och2) / 26 III 2: *qa qg* (Lbl) / 28 III 5: *qd*' *qe*'-flat (Lbl, Och1) / 32 II 1-3: *cf' qg' qa*' (Och2) / 34 III 7: o (Lcm); natural (Lbl, Och2) / 34 IV 1: *sb*d *sb*d (Lbl, Och1) / 35 IV 1: G (Och1, Och2).

Fancy no.3 (VdGS no.15)
Principal Source: Lcm (attributed).
Concordances: Och1 (attributed), Och2 (unattributed).
The title 'Fancy' appears on parts I and II of Lcm.
All the sources have partial key-signatures. The following parts have no flat in their k-s:
    part I of Och2;
    part II of Och1, Och2;
    part III of Lcm, Och1, Och2;
    part IV of Lcm, Och1.
In this edition, all parts have been written with a k-s of one flat. It has therefore been necessary to insert additional accidentals on the staves of parts III and IV. These occur before the following notes:
11 III 1, 13 III 6, 14 III 6, 15 III 1, 17 IV 7, 22 III 3, 26 IV 5, 27 III 3, 29 III 5.
Part IV is written in F4 clef in Och1 and Och2.

7 II 1-3: *b*-rest (Och1) / 13 I 5: sharp (Och1, Och2) / 17 I 7: natural (Och2) / 17 IV 7: flat (Och2) / 18 III *c*-rest: *ce*' (Och1) / 20 I 8: natural (Och1, Och2) / 22 II 1 - *m*-rest: *sb*.a' (Och2) / 22 III 3: a (Och1) / 25 I 7: o (Lcm); natural (Och1, Och2) / 26 II 10: *qa*' *qf*' (Och1) / 26 IV 4: sharp (Och1, Och2) / 28 I 2: *m* (Och1) / 28 I 3: o (Och1) / 28 II 3: natural (Och1, Och2) / 28 III 2: *qd*' *qe*' (Och1) / 29 II 5-7: *ce*' *ca*' *cf*'-natural (Och1) / 29 III 4: o (Och1) / 30 II 1-2: *cg*' *md*' (Och1) / 32 II 2: natural (Och1) / 32 III 1 - *c*-rest: *m*.g (Och2) / 33 IV 1: natural (Lcm); flat (Och1, Och2) / 34 IV 2: natural (Och1) / 36 III 6: c' (Och1, Och2) / 36 IV 2: sharp (Och1, Och2) / 36 IV 3 - 37 IV 2: *sbg sbG* (Och1) / 37 III 1-2: *sbd*' (Och1, Och2) / 37 IV 2: G (Och2).

Fancy no.4a (VdGS no.17)
Principal Source: Lcm (attributed).
Concordances: Och1 (attributed), Och2 (unattributed).
In Lcm, this fancy is found on a single loose-leaf which has been inserted and bound into the volumes directly after [Fancy no.3] (VdGS no.15). In the *Medius* book, the part was missed by the binders and therefore still appears as a fully detached leaf.
"R Mico" is written at the end of part IV in Lcm in an unknown hand. The k-s of one flat which occurs on the first stave of part II in Och1 is clearly an error and has been ignored in the Commentary.
Part IV is written in F4 clef in Och1 and Och2.

3 I 3: o (Och2) / 3 II 3-4: *c*.a' *qg*' (Och1) / 4 III 6 - *c*-rest: *m*.d' (Och1) / 6 IV 2-3: *cd*' *cd*' (Och2) / 7 II 4: *c*.c" *qc*" (Och2) / 13 II 7: o (Och1) / 15 II 6: o (all sources) / 18 IV 3: A (Och1) / 25 III 5 - 26 III 1: tied (Och1, Och2) / 26 IV 2: A (Och2) / 30 III 3: o (Och1) / 31 II 3 - 32 II 1: tied (Och1) / 32 III 2: sharp (Och1, Och2).

Fancy no.4b (VdGS no.17)
Principal Source: Lcm (attributed).
Concordances: none.
This fancy appears to be an earlier version of Fancy no.4a.

Fancy no.5 (VdGS no.16)
Principal Source: Lcm (attributed).
Concordances: Och1 (attributed), Och2 (attributed).
In Och2, this fancy is the first piece in the sequence and the parts are attributed as follows: parts I, II and III are marked "Mr Mico" and part IV is marked "Mr R Mico".
Part IV of Och1 has a k-s of two flats; all other parts in all the sources have only one flat in their k-s.
Part IV is written in F4 clef in Och1 and Och2.
In Lcm, the sharp which occurs beside the 5th note of bar 6 in part I has been suppressed in this edition because it appears to have been added by a later hand.

1 II *c*-rest: *m*-rest (Och2) / 2 II 1: o (Och1) / 4 III 1: o (Och1) / 4 III 8-9: *sbd*' (Och1, Och2) / 6 I 5: sharp (Lcm); o (Och1, Och2) / 8 IV 2: G (Och1, Och2) / 17 III 1: *me*'-flat (Och2) / 19 I 3: natural (Och2) / 19 II 1-3: *sba*' (Och1) / 19 III 5-6: *ce*' (Och1) / 20 II 3: natural (Och1, Och2) / 21 III 3: natural (Och1, Och2) / 21 III 6: *c*-rest (Och1) / 24 II 1-2: *sbd*' (Och1).

Fancy no.6 (VdGS no.1)
Principal Source: Lcm (attributed).
Concordances: Lbl (unattributed), Och1 (attributed), Och2 (unattributed).
Part I is missing in Lbl.
Each part in Och1 has "4 Partes" written in the top left-hand corner. Part I of Och1 is marked "Cantus" and part IV is marked "Bassus".
In the Commentary, the misplaced flat in the k-s of part II in Och2 is treated as if it occurs in the correct space. In part IV of Och2, the extra flat which occurs on the fourth line in the k-s of the first stave only is ignored in the Commentary.
A double barline occurs at the end of bar 21 in all parts of Lcm. In Och1, Och2 and Lbl, this point is marked with repeat signs in all parts.

16 II 4 - 17 II 1: tie om. (Lbl) / 18 III 3-5: *ca mb*-flat *ca*; correct reading added by later hand (Lbl) / 19 III 2 - 20 III 1: *mg*, *mg* tied to *cg* (Och1) / 19 IV 3: flat (Och2); natural (Lbl) / 24 II 7 - 25 II 1: tie om. (Lbl) / 36 III 5-6: om. (Och1) / 42 III 4 - 43 III 1: tied (Lbl).

Fancy no.7 (VdGS no.2)
Principal Source: Lcm (attributed).
Concordances: Lbl (unattributed), Och1 (attributed), Och2 (unattributed).
Part I is missing in Lbl.

3 III 7 - 4 III 1: tied (Lbl) / 13 III 2: o (Lbl) / 13 III 3: natural (Lbl) / 16 II 6 - 17 II 1: tie om. (Lbl) / 26 II 4: natural (Lbl) / 26 II 6: natural (Lbl) / 27 III 10: flat (Lbl) / 27 IV: extra *b*-rest (Och1) / 30 II 4: d' (Lbl) / 30 IV 2: f (Lbl) / 34 III 3 - 35 III 2: tied (Lbl) / 35 IV 3 - 36 IV 1: tied (Och2) / 36 IV 1: om. (Och1) / 37 I 5 - 38 I 1: tie om. (Och2) / 37 IV 2 - 38 IV 1: tie om. (Lbl).

Fancy no.8 (VdGS no.3)
Principal Source: Lcm (attributed).
Concordances: Lbl (unattributed), Och1 (attributed), Och2 (unattributed).
Part I is missing in Lbl.

3 I 5-6: *m*.g' (Och1) / 6 III 4-5: *cf* (Lbl) / 7 III 1: *m*.d' *cd*' (Och2) / 11 IV 8: *q*B-flat *qc* (Lbl) / 13 III 2: o (Lbl) / 13 III 3: o (Lbl) / 14 II 9-10: *qd*' *qe*' (Lbl) / 14 IV 3: *mf cf* (Lbl) / 24 III 4: o (Lbl) / 32 II 2: a' (Lbl) / 32 II 5: *m*. (Och1) / 32 IV 6 - 33 IV 1: tied (Och2) / 35 IV 4 - 36 IV 1: tie om. (Och1).

Fancy no.9 (VdGS no.4)
Principal Source: Lcm (attributed).
Concordances: Och1 (attributed), Och2 (unattributed).
The changes to C3 clefs in part IV of Och1 and Och2 for only a few notes at a time have not been noted in the Commentary.

13 III 3: e' (Och1, Och2) / 19 IV first *c*-rest: *sbc* (Och1) / 23 III 8: sharp (Och1) / 28 III 3: b (Och1) / 34 I *c*-rest: fermata om. (Och1, Och2) / 34 II 3: fermata om. (Och1, Och2) / 34 III 2: fermata om. (Och1, Och2) / 34 IV 2: fermata om. (Och1, Och2) / 37 III: extra *b*-rest (Och1) / 38 III 12,13: *q*, *c* (Och1) / 45 III 3: a (Och1).

Fancy no.10 (VdGS no.5)
Principal Source: Lcm (attributed).
Concordances: Lbl (unattributed), Och1 (attributed), Och2 (unattributed).
Part I is missing in Lbl.
Parts I and II of Lcm are labelled "Ut re mi fa".

9 III 2: o (Lbl) / 9 III 4: o (Lbl) / 15 I 4: o (Lcm, Och1); flat (Och2) / 17 I 4-7: *qf*" *qd*" *qf*" *qe*" *md*" (Och2) / 17 II 3: o (Lbl) / 17 II 3 - *m*-rest: *q*b'-flat *qa*' *c*b'-flat *ma*' (Och2) / 17 IV 4-11: *mG cD qd qe qf qe qf qd* (Och2) / 17 IV 6: o (Och1) / 18 I 4-5: *qg*" *qf*"-sharp *qg*" *qe*" (Och2) / 18 II 1-3: *qc*" *qb*' *cc*" (Och2) / 18 IV 4-5: *qc*' *qb qc*' *qa* (Och2) / 18 IV 8: o (Lbl, Och1) / 19 IV 5: o (Lbl) / 20 II 4-5: *cg*' *cf*' *cf*'-sharp (Och1) / 21 IV 1: B (Lbl) / 24 II 4: *ma*' *ca*' (Lbl) / 30 IV 2: sharp (Lbl) / 31 II 2: sharp (Lbl) / 31 III 1 - 32 III 1: tied (Och1) / 34 II 2 - 35 II 1: om. (Och1) / 35 II 2-3: tied (Och1) / 36 IV 8: o (Lbl) / 37 III 1-3: *c*.g *qa qb* (Och2) / 37 III 8: sharp (Och2) / 37 IV 4: sharp (Och1) / 38 II 5: o (Lbl) / 38 III 7: o (Och1) / 38 III 8: o (Lbl) / 38 IV 3: o (Och1, Och2) / 39 II 4: o (Och1) / 42 III 4: om. (Och1).

Fancy no.11 (VdGS no.6)
Principal Source: Lcm (attributed).
Concordances: Lbl (unattributed), Och1 (attributed), Och2 (unattributed).
Part I is missing in Lbl.
In Lcm, the sharp which occurs before the 6th note in bar 30 of part II has been suppressed in this edition because it appears to have been added by a later hand.

8 III 7: a (Och1) / 8 IV 2: o (Och2) / 8 IV 3: sharp (Och1) / 10 I *m*-rest: *sb*-rest, *m*-rest (Lcm) / 12 I 8 - 13 I 2: *ce*" tied to *ce*" (Och1, Och2) / 13 III 3,4: *m*, *c* (Och1) / 18 II 1: sharp (Lbl) / 29 II 5: o (Och1) / 30 II 6: sharp (Lcm) / 30 III 5: o (Lcm, Lbl, Och1); sharp (Och2) / 30 IV 4,5: *q*, *q* (Och1) / 30 IV 5: o (Lcm, Lbl); sharp (Och1, Och2) / 31 II 9: g (Lbl) / 31 III 8: g' (Lbl) / 33 IV 3: *qc*' *qb* (Lbl) / 34 III 8: o (Och1, Och2) / 37 II 2: *cf*'-sharp (Och2) / 37 II 5: o (all sources) / 38 IV 11 - *q*-rest: *c*.g-sharp (Lbl).

Fancy no.12 (VdGS no.7)
Principal Source: Lcm (attributed).
Concordances: Lbl (unattributed), Och1 (attributed), Och2 (unattributed).
Part I is missing in Lbl.

2 III 1: o (Lbl) / 5 III 7: sharp (Lbl) / 6 III 7,8: *q*e', *q*d'-sharp (Lbl) / 11 III 3: o (Lbl) / 11 IV 5: om. (Lbl) / 12 II 4-5: *m*g' (Och1, Och2, Lbl) / 17 I 7 - 18 I 1: tied (Och2) / 17 II 7 - 18 II 1: tied (Och2) / 22 II 1: c' (Lbl) / 22 IV: extra *b*-rest (Lbl) / 23 II *c*-rest: *m*-rest (Och1) / 23 IV 2: sharp (Lbl) / 23 IV 3: o (Lbl) / 25 II 2: c'' (Lbl) / 27 II 12: *c* (Och2) / 27 III 4-5: *m*e' (Och2) / 30 I 1: g'' (Och1) / 33 III 7: o (Lbl) / 33 IV 5: o (all sources).

Fancy no.13 (VdGS no.8)
Principal Source: Lcm (attributed).
Concordances: Lbl (unattributed), Och1 (attributed), Och2 (unattributed).
Part I is missing in Lbl.
Part II is written in the treble clef in Lbl.

7 II 1-2: *c*g' (Och2) / 13 II 10: o (all sources) / 13 IV 8: o (Lbl, Och1, Och2) / 14 III 2: o (Och1) / 17 II 1: o (Och1) / 22 IV 1: *sb*g *sb*g (Lbl, Och1, Och2) / 24 I 4 - 25 I 2: *sb*c'' *sb*c'' (Och1, Och2) / 25 III 6: f' (Lbl) / 26 III 1: f' (Lbl) / 29 II 1 - *q*-rest: *c*.g' (Lbl) / 30 IV 4: o (Lcm, Och1, Och2); flat (Lbl) / 31 IV 6: o (Och1) / 32 I 1: o (Och1) / 35 III 1: o (Lbl) / 35 III 3: o (Lcm, Lbl, Och1); flat (Och2) / 36 II 5: o (Lbl) / 36 II 6: c'' (Lbl) / 36 II 7: o (Lcm, Lbl, Och1); flat (Och2) / 36 III 2: o (Och1) / 38 II 8: o (Lcm, Och1, Och2); flat (Lbl) / 38 III 8: o (Lcm, Och1); flat (Lbl, Och2).

Fancy no.14 (VdGS no.9)
Principal Source: Lcm (attributed).
Concordances: Lbl (unattributed), Och1 (attributed), Och2 (unattributed).
Part I is missing in Lbl.

10 II 11 - 11 II 1: tie om. (Lbl, Och1, Och2) / 12 III 8: o (Lbl) / 13 IV 3,4: *q*., *sq* (Lbl) / 17 II 8: f' (Lbl) / 18 I 8: o (Och1) / 19 II 6: o (Lbl) / 20 IV 7: flat (Och1, Och2) / 21 I 3: o (Och2) / 24 II 7: o (Lbl) / 24 II 9: o (Lbl, Och1) / 25 IV 6: o (Och1); *q*B-flat, *q*G (Lbl) / 26 III 6: o (Och1) / 30 III 1, 2: *q*, *q* (Lbl) / 32 II 11 - 33 II 1: tie om. (Lbl) / 32 III 3: o (Och1) / 33 II 2: *sq*g'-sharp *sq*f'-sharp (Lbl) / 33 II 8: a' (Lbl) / 33 III 4-5: *c*d' (Lbl) / 34 II 9: o (all sources) / 34 IV 1 - *q*-rest: *c*.a (Lbl) / 36 III 3: o (Lcm); flat (Lbl, Och1, Och2) / 37 II 1 - *q*-rest: *c*.e' (Lbl) / 39 III 5: o (Lbl) / 39 III 10,11: *q*., *sq* (Lbl, Och1, Och2) / 40 I 2: o (Lbl) / 40 IV 1: c (Lbl) / 43 IV 1: D (Och2).

Fancy no.15 (VdGS no.10)
Principal Source: Lcm (attributed).
Concordances: Lbl (unattributed), Och1 (attributed), Och2 (unattributed).
Part I is missing in Lbl.

3 III 1,2: *m*., *c* (Och2) / 13 II 5: f'-sharp (Lbl) / 14 IV 9: o (Och1) / 22 III 2: o (Lbl) / 23 III 5: o (Lbl, Och1) / 23 IV 3 - *sb*-rest: *sb*d *m*-rest (Lbl) / 24 I 5: o (all sources) / 24 III 2: o (Lbl) / 25 IV 1: b (Och1) / 27 II 8: o (Lbl) / 27 II 10: o (Lbl, Och1) / 27 III 7: o (Lbl) / 28 III 7: a (Lbl) / 28 IV 2: o (Lbl) / 30 III 9: o (Lbl) / 31 II 5: o (Och1) / 32 IV 5: *c*d *q*d (Lbl) / 34 III 15 - 35 III 1: *c*d' tied to *q*d' followed by *q*d' (Lbl) / 36 II 3: *q* (Och1) / 38 IV 3 - 39 IV 1: *m*G tied to *c*G followed by *q*F-sharp *q*E (Och1, Och2).

Fancy no.16 (VdGS no.11)
Principal Source: Lcm (attributed).
Concordances: Lbl (attributed), Och1 (attributed), Och2 (unattributed).
Part I is missing in Lbl.
In Lbl, this fancy is the first piece in the sequence and the end of part IV is marked "R. Mico".

2 I 2: *c*.c'' *q*c'' (Och2) / 7 IV 5: o (Och1) / 15 II 3 - 18 II 2: om. (Och1) / 17 II 11 - 18 II 1: tie om. (Lbl) / 17 III 1: a (Lbl) / 23 II 2-3: *m*b'-flat (Lbl, Och1, Och2) / 24 IV *m*-rest: om. (Och1) / 27 II 4-5: *c*f' (Lbl) / 28 II 6,7: g', f'-sharp (Lbl) / 28 III 1: *c*-rest (Lbl) / 28 IV 1: *sb*d *sb*d (Lbl) / 29 III 1: *m*g *c*g (Lbl) / 29 III 3: o (Och2) / 30 III 9: o (Lcm, Och1); flat (Lbl, Och2) / 30 III 3 - 31 III 1: tie om. (Lbl) / 30 IV 4 - 31 IV 1: tie om. (Och1).

Fancy no.17 (VdGS no.12)
Principal Source: Lcm (attributed).
Concordances: Lbl (unattributed), Och1 (attributed), Och2 (unattributed).
Part I is missing in Lbl.

1 III 3: o (Och1) / 3 III 3: o (Lcm, Och1); flat (Lbl, Och2) / 6 IV 10: o (Och1) / 8 II 5: o (Och1) / 13 III 9: o (Och1) / 15 IV 7: flat (Lbl) / 15 IV 13: o (all sources) / 19 IV 7: d (Lbl) / 20 IV 7: o (Lbl) / 20 IV 13: o (Och1) / 22 I 6: fermata (Och2) / 22 II 2: fermata (Och2) / 22 III 3: o (Och1) / 22 III 4: fermata (Och2) / 25 II 3-6: *m*e'-flat *sb*g (Lbl) / 26 III 1-2: *sb*.a-flat (Och2) / 29 I 5: o (Lbl) / 31 IV 1: *sb*G *sb*G (Och2).

Fancy no.18 (VdGS no.[18])
Principal Source: Och2.
Concordances: none.
No comment.

Fancy no.19 (VdGS no.[19])
Principal Source: Och2.
Concordances: none.
Repeat signs occur at the end of bar 23 in parts II, III and IV. The same place is marked by double barlines in part I. In this edition, the final notes of the section in bar 23 have been standardized in each part to fit the barring.

38 IV 7: *c*

Pavan no.1 (VdGS no.1)
Principal Source: Lcm (attributed).
Concordance: Lms (unattributed).
The title 'Pavan' is given on each part of Lcm.
The changes in time-signature at bars 5 and 16 are editorial.

14 III 7: o (Lcm); flat (Lms).

Pavan no.2 (VdGS no.2)
Principal Source: Lcm (attributed).
Concordance: Lms (unattributed).

4 II 2: natural (Lms) / 10 II 1: *sb* (all sources) / 12 III 3: natural (Lms).

Pavan no.3 (VdGS no.3)
Principal Source: Lcm (attributed).
Concordance: Lms (unattributed).

7 III : extra *sb*e' after note 4 (Lcm); om. (Lms).

Pavan no.4 (VdGS no.4)
Principal Source: Lcm (attributed).
Concordance: Lms (unattributed).
In Lcm, the sharps which occur above the fourth note in bar 19 of part III and beside the first note in bar 20 of part IV have been suppressed in this edition because they appear to have been added by a later hand.

19 III 4: sharp (Lcm); o (Lms) / 20 IV 1: sharp (Lcm); o (Lms) / 23 III 4-6: slurred (Lms).

Meredith Tyler © 1997, Sydney, Australia

[Fancy No.1]

[Fancy No.2]

[Fancy No.3]

[Fancy No.4a]

©1997 Fretwork Editions   Richard Mico: The Four-Part Consort Music, edited by Meredith Tyler

[Fancy No.4b]

©1997 Fretwork Editions   Richard Mico: The Four-Part Consort Music, edited by Meredith Tyler

[Fancy No.5]

[Fancy No.6]

[Fancy No.7]

[Fancy No.8]

[Fancy No.9]

©1997 Fretwork Editions   Richard Mico: The Four-Part Consort Music, edited by Meredith Tyler

[Fancy No.10]

©1997 Fretwork Editions   Richard Mico: The Four-Part Consort Music, edited by Meredith Tyler

[Fancy No.11]

©1997 Fretwork Editions   Richard Mico: The Four-Part Consort Music, edited by Meredith Tyler

[Fancy No.12]

[Fancy No.13]

©1997 Fretwork Editions   Richard Mico: The Four-Part Consort Music, edited by Meredith Tyler

[Fancy No.14]

[Fancy No.15]

©1997 Fretwork Editions   Richard Mico: The Four-Part Consort Music, edited by Meredith Tyler

[Fancy No.16]

©1997 Fretwork Editions   Richard Mico: The Four-Part Consort Music, edited by Meredith Tyler

[Fancy No.17]

[Fancy No.18]

©1997 Fretwork Editions   Richard Mico: The Four-Part Consort Music, edited by Meredith Tyler

[Fancy No.19]

[Pavan No.1]

Page left blank to avoid a page-turn

[Pavan No.2]

47

[Pavan No.3]

[Pavan No.4]

©1997 Fretwork Editions   Richard Mico: The Four-Part Consort Music, edited by Meredith Tyler

www.ingramcontent.com/pod-product-compliance
Lightning Source LLC
Chambersburg PA
CBHW042307300426
44110CB00045B/2836